AVAILABLE

By Rich Garza

with Greg Singleton

 First printing 2014
Printed in the United States of America

Library of Congress data:

Rich Garza (1958 -)
Available

Greg Singleton (1952 -)
Available

ISBN-10:
0615983383

ISBN-13:
978-0-615-98338-7

Foreword

By Paul Eshleman
Vice President, Campus Crusade for Christ

One of the great untold stories in professional football is the impact made off the field by countless players and coaches. Whether they achieve great fame or not, the mark they leave on society are lives of young men and women who have been challenged to live a quality of life far beyond the Super bowl.

In this book, Rich Garza tells us his story from the inside. His refreshing and honest account of his struggles, his questions and his eventual commitment to God is inspiring and heartwarming.

As the National Football League was gaining prominence in the 1970s there were very few players that talked openly about their faith and their personal lives. Bill Glass led a Bible study for the Cleveland Browns, Raymond Berry and Don Shinnick were active in faith-based efforts and Bart Starr led the Packers in the Lord's Prayer before each game.

During those years, my father, Doc Eshleman, came in contact with a number of players who said that for at least half of the year they could not attend church because of pre-game meetings, taping and travel to the stadium. The

Atlanta Falcons and the Miami Dolphins became the first teams to establish a voluntary chapel service. It was usually held in a meeting room at the hotel where they were staying, half an hour before the pre-game meal.

One of the early adopters of the pre-game chapel service was Coach George Allen of the Los Angeles Rams. Allen at the time was also General Manager of the Rams. In the winter meeting of GMs from all over the league, one of the executives began quizzing Allen about this new innovation. He said something like, "George, you'll do anything to win. I hear you've got a prayer meeting going on Sundays now." Allen responded to the jibe very seriously. "Yes", he said,"that is my chapel service. It's the one thing I wouldn't change even if, God forbid, we had a losing season. By the time these men get to the NFL, they know 98% of all the football they are ever gonna know. It's my job to get them to play together. It's tough to coach togetherness, but my chapel service brings my white guys and my black guys together." In the next week, almost every GM across the league called Doc Eshleman to ask him to set up a chapel on their team. The inspiration Rich Garza received in those chapel services, he has since passed on to millions of students in assemblies Though most of us will never remember his athletic accomplishments, there are hundreds of thousands of students who look back on his talks at their school as a pivotal point in their lives.

In those few moments Rich Garza became their friend, their confidant and pointed the way toward hope for the future.

1 Living My Dreams

"When I was a child, I spoke and thought and reasoned as a child. But when I grew up, I put away childish things. Now we see things imperfectly, like puzzling reflections in a mirror, but then we will see everything with perfect clarity. All that I know now is partial and incomplete, but then I will know everything completely, just as God now knows me completely."
I Corinthians 13:11-12

It was almost surreal. Had it not been for the fact that I had worked so hard to get to this place, it would have been exactly like hundreds of dreams that I had during my lifetime. I was a pro football player, and my team, the Philadelphia Stars, was playing for the championship. In the tunnel, right before we moved on to the field, I took one second to drink it all in. The sights, the sounds, and even the smells were just like I had always imagined they would be. Then, I heard the stadium announcer's voice blast through the stadium. "At left guard, from Temple University, Rich Garza!" I trotted to midfield to join my teammates. The cameras from ABC Sports and ESPN zoomed into my face, and I tried to manage that tough look that would intimidate my opponents. But, truthfully, I was so excited that I didn't know whether I was going to laugh or cry.

As great as that moment was, had this all taken place just a few months earlier, the feelings would have been even more intense for me. But, on this day of the first United States Football League championship, my life was in the middle of a transformation. This moment was something that

FROM ANY PART OF THE CITY
the steel mills and iron factories were at the heart of Bethlehem, Pennsylvania.

I had lived my entire life for. It felt really great to be experiencing it, but my whole perspective had been changing over the past few weeks. It was just like I had been a blind man for the first twenty-five years of my life, and suddenly, I was waking up to a whole new world. I was seeing my story in a completely different way.

Bethlehem, Pennsylvania, was a great place for a tough guy to grow up. My dad's father, Brigido Garza, left Mexico when he was a young man to work in Bethlehem's steel industry. And, John Morga, my grandfather on my mom's side, was from a family of Polish and Russian immigrants.

He was an ironworker in Bethlehem. Both of my grandpas were solid, sturdy men who worked hard to bring their families a better life.

Like most other families in the city, we lived and breathed the iron and steel industry. Working in those factories was sweaty, backbreaking work. It shaped the attitudes and beliefs of everyone in Bethlehem. A man was expected to work hard to take care of his family, because that's what God expected of him. That was Bethlehem's mission statement and her faith.

My dad, Richard Garza Sr., started out as an ironworker, but he had one thing he just couldn't overcome – a fear of high places. And climbing and balancing like a tightrope walker was required. So all his co-workers teased him about it until he had to make a change. He went to work for his boyhood friend, Ripper, managing a sports bar before sports bars were a thing. The Beef Baron was full of television sets tuned to any sports even that happened to be on the air. In those days before cable and satellite dishes, viewers had to depend on antennas to pick up the few stations that were available. Open-face steak sandwiches, sausage sandwiches and the best burgers you ever sank your teeth in made up the menu. The place was open from noon until late at night, and, Dad had to take care of the evening crowd. They'd stay open very late, and he was there until the last customer decided it was time to go home. Long weeks were normal. In fact, they were necessary. With all that, none of us kids ever felt neglected, and he never missed a game we played.

My dad was a very good man, and he worked so hard. His love for me, his oldest son, and for my mom, my three brothers and my sister was expressed through his hard work. What I learned from him was what I saw in him – be tough and work hard.

While Dad was our strength, Jean, my mom,

FAMILY TIES

Here's my brother, Bob (middle), with our grandfathers, Brigido Garza (left), and John Morga (right).

was the soul of our family. She made certain that we had every advantage we could afford in order for all the Garza kids to learn and achieve. A stay-at-home mother, she sacrificed everything for the sake of our family.

"Remember, you're the best!" I heard Mom tell me that a million times. Even today, when I talk to her about my plans or my thoughts, my family or my ministry, she still tells me that. She assured every one of her kids with that all the time. Because she told us that so often and so sincerely, we believed it.

When there was an opportunity for recreation for the Garza family, it was found on the football fields, baseball fields and basketball courts of Bethlehem. And, if you were going to be a good athlete, then, of course, you needed to work hard. Our family was all about sports. We watched them, we talked about them and we played them. When I was just a child, I began showing an interest in sports, and my whole family encouraged it. So the more they appreciated it, the harder I worked. And the harder I worked, the more success I had. Somehow I got it in my head and in my heart that if I could climb that ladder all the way to the top, a career in professional football, I would have achieved everything. If I made it there, I would have all the money I needed, all the attention I wanted, and I would be accepted in every circle. Life would be complete, and I would be totally content and satisfied. So that became not only my goal, but my passion.

I started playing organized team football in the seventh grade at Northeast Junior High School. Once I got a taste of competition and achievement, I was hooked. I wanted to play every sport, all the time. So I went out for basketball, track and baseball, at Northeast, too. All year long, almost every week, I had a game. I loved looking in the stands and seeing my Mom and Dad there, along with the rest of the family.

The most satisfying moment of my junior high years happened at the football banquet when I was in ninth grade. For three years, Northeast Junior High was undefeated, and my last year, I was named the team's Most Valuable Player. My coach, Joe Craig, was probably my favorite coach of all time. That evening, he had me come to the front of the room, and while people applauded, he handed me a trophy and shook my hand. Getting that kind of recognition brought on a

FAMILY PORTRAIT

Family was so important to all of us in the Garza family. On the top row are my brother Ron, me, my sister, Jean, and my brother Bob. On the bottom row are my dad, Rich, my mom, Jean, and my youngest brother, Ross. I love these people!

PROUD PARENTS

Mom and Dad were so proud of me when I won the MVP Award at the Northeast Junior High School football banquet. I was 14 years old and in the ninth grade, and up until that time, this was probably the happiest day of my life.

flood of emotion inside me. My heart was beating so hard in my chest that I thought it would explode. I remember the smiles on my parents' faces and the tears in my mom's eyes. I could tell that I had made them proud of me, and that was the best feeling in the world. If this felt so good in ninth grade, I could only imagine how great things would be when I made it to the pros.

As I moved on to Liberty High School, I couldn't wait to try out for the football team. The coaches knew who I was, and they greeted me with how glad they were to have me there. As big as the plans were that they had for me, mine were even bigger. I wanted to be the best that the Liberty Hurricanes had ever seen. That was not going to be an easy task. NFL Hall of Famer, Chuck Bednarik graduated from Liberty before making it big with the Philadelphia Eagles. And, my hero, Mike Hartenstine, played for Liberty, too. When I began high school, Mike was a star with the Chicago Bears. I had big dreams, and I was going to do whatever I had to do achieve them.

Even though football was my greatest love, I wanted more than just fall competition. So just like in junior high, I tried out for almost every sport that the school had to offer. Three years and ten varsity letters later, I graduated, and was ready to move on to bigger and better things. But, I was going to miss all my friends, coaches and teammates. My best buddies, Pit, Jimbo, Chuck and Kyle were all doing other things and going other places. I would never forget them, though.

But, for the first time in my football life, I was on the brink of a big disappointment. With the success I had in high school, I expected the big colleges to be beating down the doors, wanting me to be a part of their program. A few smaller schools reached out to me recruiting me to be a part of their football team. But the big name schools, like Penn State, Notre Dame and Ohio State, the programs that would give me the inside track into the pros, never did much more than send me a letter. The NCAA had put a 30-scholarship limit on all the Division 1 schools, and, at 230 pounds, I was not big enough to be one of the few linemen that were recruiting.

Didn't they know the plans that I'd made? Weren't they aware of what a hard worker I was? Had they just not watched the game film closely enough? I was disappointed, but it spurred me on to pursue my dreams even more fiercely. Wherever I ended up playing college football, they were going to see a bigger and better Rich Garza. I was determined to succeed.

INSTANT REPLAY

You can watch ABC Sports' telecast of the first USFL Championship game at...

https://vimeo.com/84631010

I'm number 61, at left guard!

2 Flying High with the Owls

"I know every bird of the mountains, and everything that moves in the field is Mine."
Psalm 50:11

Just when I was about to run out of patience and time with my college football future, I got a phone call. On the other end of the line was the former coach of Liberty's biggest rival, Bethlehem Catholic High School. He had just accepted the position as offensive line coach at Temple University, and he was looking for football players.

"Rich, I know you're a good lineman and we could really use you here at Temple. If you're willing to walk on here your freshman year, and if you can produce the way I think you can, I'm pretty sure I can get you a scholarship by year two."

That was all I needed to hear. Temple was in Philadelphia, about an hour's drive from home, so my family could easily travel to see my games. And, the Owls had a great football tradition. Glenn "Pop" Warner, one of college football's most famous coaches, led the team back in the 30's. Temple boasted of a long line of All-Americans who had been successful in the pros. Defensive tackle Joe Klecko, who would become an All-Pro performer with the New York Jets, had just been named All-American and was coming back to the Owls for his senior season. The most famous Owl football player of all time, though, never played in the NFL. Bill Cosby was a fullback for Temple in 1961-1962, before leaving school to launch his comedy career. I think he made a good choice.

Temple University offered me a great opportunity to continue my football career. The head coach was Wayne Hardin, who, in 1977, was in the middle of the finest coaching stint the Temple Owls had ever seen. He had arrived there in 1970, after an impressive run as head coach at the United States Naval Academy. He had coached two Heisman Trophy winners at Navy, running back Joe Bellino and quarterback Roger Staubach. Since he began his stint at Temple he had put together an impressive 42-23-1 record.

The Owls weren't in a conference than, so they played an independent schedule that, every year allowed them to take on some of that decade's biggest football powerhouses in the country. Penn State, Syracuse, West Virginia, and Pittsburgh were all regular opponents and usually came into the game ranked in the Top Twenty.

I was confident that I could make it there, though. I determined that I was going to give everything I could do to convince Coach Hardin and the rest of the staff that I deserved a football scholarship. Whatever they asked of me, I was going to do, and even more. My mom had always told me that I was the best. I believed it, and I was going to prove it.

The step up from high school football to college football is huge. During my first year, every day as an Owl was a challenge, and it took my entire effort and absolute focus. As it began to pay off, I worked even harder. The coaches decided it would best for me to redshirt my first season, but, by the third week, they had placed me on the travelling squad. I was able to take in every game, we played. That was huge for my football education. I watched and I learned. I worked out, and I got bigger and stronger.

As my second season, my redshirt freshman year, began, I had won a starting position on the offensive line. We finished the year with a 5-5-1 record and earned a trip to Tokyo, Japan, to play in the Mirage Bowl against quarterback Doug Williams and the Grambling Tigers. And, by the time that 1977 season ended, I was a Temple football letterman. True to their word, the coaching staff rewarded me with a full athletic scholarship. It seemed that I was back on track now, headed toward my goal of playing pro football.

Then, suddenly, I was blindsided by something I hadn't expected. I had forgotten what the purpose of college really was, and when grades came out in the spring, I was faced with an ultimatum. I had to do better in the classroom or I wouldn't be able to play football. It was a huge dose of reality for a 19-year old guy who had his priorities completely messed up. College, to me, was a means of playing football. My only focus about academics was that I would do what I had to do remain eligible. That's my biggest regret about my time at Temple. I wish I had taken advantage of what was offered to me there, excellent professors who were all about increasing students' opportunities and perspectives. My first thought when I considered my class schedule each semester was that I would pick whatever was going to be easy. And, looking back, that cost me so much in becoming what I could have been as a student.

With my academic eligibility hanging by a thread, my sophomore football season rolled around. I was entrenched as a starting offensive guard, and already I was expected to provide leadership to the new guys on the team. We fought to a solid 7-3-1 record that year, and defeated Boston College 28-24 in a return trip to Mirage Bowl. Everyone on the team sensed that this was just the beginning of something special. And, here I was, an integral part of what Coach

ALMA MATER

The Temple University campus is located on the edge of downtown Philadelphia.

Hardin and the Temple Owls were building. I had the last half of my college football experience ahead of me, and, if it went just as I had planned, my dream of a career in pro football was right in my sights. Deep inside me, the hunger was becoming more intense. Despite the success I was achieving on the field, I felt an emptiness and a lack of satisfaction with what was going on in my life. More than ever, I reasoned that once I was a pro football player, the money and the recognition would make me happy.

As we entered the 1979 season, we had the attention of college football experts. They predicted that Temple University would be a powerhouse in the East. And in the first three games of the season, we didn't disappoint them. We easily defeated West Virginia, Drake and Delaware, giving us a 3-0 record and a ranking in the

IMPRESSIVE

I was powerlifting during the off-season at Temple, and this is what I looked like when I was squatting 601 pounds.

Top Twenty in the nation.

Next on our schedule was our long-time rival, the University of Pittsburgh Panthers. Their freshman quarterback was Dan Marino, who would do even bigger things later, during his NFL career. The Panthers had come into the season ranked #5 in the nation, but the week before, they had been upset by the University of North Carolina. And they weren't happy. Our offense never could get in gear, and they edged us out, 10-9.

We answered that disappointing loss with five consecutive wins, and with the bowl picture beginning to come into focus, it appeared that we were destined for a post-season game. After a loss to highly-ranked Penn State, we crushed Villanova, to end our regular season at 9-2. I had had a very good season, and felt that I had contributed to our team's success. Our offensive line, nicknamed the Broad Street Wrecking Crew, was as good as almost any in the country. Coach Joe Paterno at Penn State said he had never seen any better.

We were invited to the Garden State Bowl in New Jersey, on December 15. Our opponent was the University of California, who represented the Pac-10 Conference with a 7-4 record. It was a cold day in East Rutherford, and many of the fans who had bought tickets decided not to brave the sub-freezing temperatures.

The Owls' quarterback, Brian Broomell, and our top receiver, Gerald "Sweet Feet" Lucear, had been a great combination all year long. In this game, they were clicking again. I was feeling very good about my performance, too. The offensive line was giving Brian plenty of time to find his receivers, and we were opening up huge holes for our running backs, Kevin Duckett and Mark Bright, to blast through. At the end of the first quarter, we had a commanding 21-0 lead.

Good teams don't give up though. California came back fighting, and closed the gap to 21-14 at the half. As the fourth quarter began, the Golden Bears kicked a field goal to make the game a real contest, 21-17. But, then, Broomell and Lucear hooked up again on a seven-yard touchdown pass to put it away for us.

I remember how great it felt, celebrating in the locker room after the win. My teammates congratulated me on the work I had done, letting me know that my play had been a key to our success. Mark Bright, our running back, was named Most Valuable Player in the game, rushing for 112 yards on 19 carries, many of them directly a result of the great job our offensive line had done.

Paul Zimmerman, one of Sports Illustrated's most respected writers was covering the game, and pressed his way through the crowd of reporters to my locker. "Hey, Garza. I think you ought to know that you got my vote for MVP. You did a great job opening all those holes." That was one of the biggest compliments I ever received in my football career. Rarely did an offensive lineman get the recognition that was usually reserved for the backs and receivers. To hear that someone like Zimmerman appreciated my hard work enough to cast his MVP vote for me was a thrill.

As the coaches and players reflected on the great year, they handed out the team awards for the entire season. Our offensive line, known as the Broad Street Wrecking Crew, was named the team's MVP, and the recognition from my teammates and coaches was the best feeling in the world.

As my last football season at Temple began, I had one last chance to make the pro scouts believe in me. I was unanimously elected by my teammates as one of the captains of the 1980 squad, and that was a real honor. The team had some question marks, though. So many of our key players, including quarterback Brian Broomell, had graduated. That meant that those of us who had been around awhile had the responsibility of bringing this team together. As hard as we tried, it seemed like nothing ever meshed that year. Sometimes, the parts just don't fit, and we struggled through a disappointing 4-7 season. Once again, I was named Outstanding Offensive Lineman, and finished my college career with four varsity letters. But that just didn't seem as exciting in light of how we performed as a team.

My memories of Temple University, my friends, my coaches and my teammates, are sweet. It was a place where, in so many ways, I matured. I appreciate all the people who took the time and effort to have input into my life. My offensive line coach, Carmen Piccone was an amazing influence on me. There were a group of guys there that I played with that were like brothers to me – Sting, Pokey Joe, Curs, Iggszy, Fitz, Puggs, Big Bear, Broo Dink, T.G., Detito, and Okie. That last spring, with Temple in my rear-view mirror, I was on the threshold of the biggest opportunity of my whole life, the thing that I had dreamed about. I had done everything I could do to prepare for it. Now, with the NFL draft just ahead, I could only hope that the scouts had noticed.

HISTORY MAKER

Our coach, Wayne Hardin, had an 80-52-3 record at Temple, the best in school history.

3 Welcome to the NFL

"Though he fall, he shall not be utterly cast down; for the Lord *upholds him with His hand." Psalm 37:24*

The first step in the transition from college football to the NFL is finding an agent. I chose Tony Agnone, a sharp, young attorney who was starting to make a name for himself in the sports agent world. Tony was based in Maryland, not very far from Philadelphia. When I walked into his office, I was so excited about the future. I sat down across the desk from Tony and waited to hear his plan.

"Rich, I'm going to be honest with you," he said. "There are plenty of good offensive lineman in this draft. And Temple didn't have the kind of year that they had a season ago. You guys just didn't get much attention this year." My anticipation was beginning to fade a bit as he talked. "I'll do everything I can do for you, but I don't think we can expect that any team will draft you." I'm sure I had a shocked expression on my face. "Now, if you had come out early and been eligible for the draft last year, it might be a different story. After the great job you did then, along with the Owls' record, and the outstanding game you had in the Garden State Bowl, you were on all the teams' radar. You probably would have been drafted."

I walked away from that place determined that my dreams to be a pro football player weren't going to end this way, at this time and at this place. I second-guessed myself, disappointed that I had thought one more year would have improved my status. There were a hundred "what ifs" running through my mind.

I went back to Philadelphia and continued to prepare to be an NFL lineman, despite my agent's bad news. On draft day, I settled in by the phone, and waited. And, waited. And, waited. When the draft was over, and my name wasn't called, I closed my eyes and laid my head back and thought, "What now?" I knew I was meant to play pro football. The one thing that I thought would make me complete had hit a huge roadblock. This was supposed to be the time I had imagined I would be settled and established. And, now, I realized that my emotions were playing with me. I was going from high to low, top to bottom, and full to empty. It wasn't a feeling that I was used to, and it was certainly not one that I enjoyed.

The phone ringing ended my self-examination, and when I answered it, Tony was on the line. "Well, Rich, the draft didn't happen for you," he said. "But I have some really great news. The Eagles are interested in taking a look at you in training camp in the summer."

The Philadelphia Eagles were my team. I had grown up with them, watching their games, and reading about their players. Now I had a chance to wear that uniform – the green and silver. The previous season, Coach Dick Vermeil led the Eagles all the way to the Super Bowl, where they fell to the Oakland Raiders. Now, I had a chance to be the guy that quarterback Ron Jaworski depended on to keep the defense off him. I was going to be reunited with roommate at Temple, Mike Curcio, who had just finished his rookie year at linebacker with the Eagles.

I arrived in training camp the summer of 1981, and I was on a mission. I had never worked harder in my life. I was passionate about being a Philadelphia Eagle, and the coaches were seeing the best Rich Garza had to offer. In practice sessions and in the first two pre-season games, they noticed. I was constantly getting good feedback from the staff, and I was beginning to feel like I belonged.

The third pre-season game was against the New Orleans Saints. When the starting lineups were posted that week, my name was listed at left guard. I responded to the faith that the coaches had put in me with a great performance. Everyone congratulated me on the game, and, that added fuel to the fire.

As we were on the field stretching before the fourth pre-season game against the Jets, Coach Vermeil walked up to me and put his hands on my shoulders. He looked me right in the eyes and said, "Rich, you have what it takes to be an Eagle." For the first time, I really felt a part of this team.

I wasn't scheduled to play that night because the staff was going to focus on some of the veteran linemen who had been under-performing. But there was only one more cut to be made to get us down to the 45-player limit. I was almost certain that, after my performance against the Saints, and with what Coach Vermeil had said to me, I would be offered a contract with the Philadelphia Eagles.

But, pro football is fickle. The next day, they announced the final cuts, and my name was on the list. I never understood how I got from "having what it takes" to being cut from the Eagles in a matter of one short week. I just knew that I was made to play pro football, if not here, then for someone else.

For the first time since seventh grade, I had a fall without football. It was a frustrating situation to be in. I watched football games live and on television, and I wanted to be out on that field so badly it almost hurt. I had almost a whole year to get bigger, faster, stronger and better. I knew what it took to do that, so I just had to reach down within myself to find the discipline to make it happen.

Right after the 1982 draft, Tony called me with some good news. The Denver Broncos were interested in seeing me. I packed up my bags and headed to the Mile High City, ready for a new challenge. I had solid performances in the first two pre-season contests, then, I broke three ribs, keeping me out of workouts, and landing me on the injured reserve list. I was a forgotten man while I sat on the sidelines that week. I watched the next game in street clothes. Just like the last season, we got down to the last cut. When the final 45-man roster was announced, the Broncos decided to let me go.

I would have expected to have been devastated by the news. But, surprisingly, I was still confident that there was a place for me. I knew I was a good football player. The experience of these two NFL camps just assured me that I was so close to seeing my dreams come true. Somewhere there was a team who would recognize that I would fit right in to their program, and someday, I would know what it felt like to be fulfilled.

NFL GAME

I played my first home professional football game at Veterans' Stadium with the Philadelphia Eagles. I would soon find out that pro football is often tougher to handle off the field than during the games.

4 Now I See

"One thing I know: that though I was blind, now I see." John 9:25

Something was stirring in the pro football world. It had been a while since the NFL's dominance had been challenged, but there was a new kid on the block who was making a lot of noise. In 1982, The United States Football League announced that they would award twelve franchises and play a full schedule beginning in the spring of 1983.

When Heisman Trophy winner Herschel Walker left the University of Georgia after his junior year, and signed with the New Jersey Generals, the USFL had immediate credibility. They reached an agreement with ABC Sports and a new sports network, ESPN, to televise their games. And, some top NFL players began to jump to the new spring league. Over the next three years, Jim Kelly, Reggie White and other greats would wear USFL uniforms.

When they started signing players before the first season, I got a call from my agent, and he was excited. "Are you ready to go to the USFL?" Tony asked. The Philadelphia Stars called and they're definitely interested in you."

Carl Petersen had been Director of Player Personnel for the Eagles when I almost made their final roster. He had been hired as the Stars' General Manager, and knowing that I was a local Temple guy, he was eager to sign me. When I talked to him, I couldn't believe what I was hearing. "Rich," he said, "we want to sign you to a guaranteed, no-cut contract with the Stars." And,

VICTORY IS SWEET

After a big victory over Hershel Walker and the New Jersey Generals, I'm savoring the win on the

then, he told me the salary and I almost passed out.

This was it. I had achieved what I had always wanted. I was a professional football player, making a very good salary. It wasn't going to end in training camp, either. For a few days, I was on an emotional high, but I didn't feel exactly like I thought I would. It didn't take long for that empty feeling to return, and I couldn't figure out why.

Once I got to the Stars' training camp, the football part of me was having a great time. From my point of view, the Stars looked like a very good football team. Jim Mora, our coach, was a smart, fiery guy, who would later have a lot of success as a coach in the NFL. He knew exactly what he wanted from the team and from each individual player. It was a pleasure to play for him.

Our quarterback was former Penn State All-American Chuck Fusina, who had been with the

STARS PLAYER

I was the starting offensive guard for the Stars. Here I am in action against the Birmingham Stallions.

NFL's Tampa Bay Buccaneers the previous three seasons. Two rookies who had been college All-Americans had significant roles as well. Kelvin Bryant had starred at North Carolina, and, on the offensive line was former UCLA tackle, Irv Eatman.

I was listed as the starting left guard as we began the first week of USFL football against the Denver Gold. My return to Colorado was under much better circumstances than when I had left several months before. I was back as a starter for the Philadelphia Stars, and the game was on ABC before a national audience.

The game was a tight defensive struggle, but we scratched out a 13-7 victory. It was a bit disappointing that the offense didn't put many points on the scoreboard, but it was great to get a win in the first game.

The Philadelphia Stars proved to be a very good football team. Through the first eight weeks of the season, we were 7-1, and I had remained the starter every game. The coaches and my teammates had confidence in me. I was playing well, but, inside, I will still searching for the contentment that should have come along with the success. Where was the peace and the gratification?

Going into our Week 9 game against Coach

Steve Spurrier's Tampa Bay Bandits, we were on a roll. Our only loss of the year had been to the Bandits five weeks earlier, and we couldn't wait to get another shot at them. As the week went on, our anticipation was beginning to build, and by the time we boarded our flight to Florida, we were focused.

On April 30, I woke up in the hotel room with nothing but that game on my mind. Each week, I could put aside the inner conflicts I had for the sake of football. I had a game day ritual. I followed the same routine every week, eating the same food and doing the same tasks all day. Part of my ritual was attending the team chapel service held before every game. It wasn't that I felt that I needed some spiritual enrichment. It was just like a rabbit's foot to me, something I needed to do for good luck before the game.

I had never been a religious person. Growing up in the Garza home, we attended church on Sundays when I was very young, but I couldn't stand it. It was so boring to me when I was a kid. I actually did pray every Sunday morning, though. My prayer was that my dad wouldn't wake up in time for us to go to church. The times I heard him in his room snoring, when that "zero hour" arrived, I felt like maybe there really was a God and he actually heard me that week. By the time our house was full of kids, and

LIFE CHANGER

When I first saw Ira "Doc" Eshelman at the chapel service in Tampa, I never imagined the impact that he would have on my life. He not only introduced me to a relationship with Christ, he also became my mentor and one of my best friends.

MAKING A WAY

Running back Kelvin Bryant follows me through a hole in the Birmingham defense.

we were all totally involved in sports, church had faded into the background.

I walked into that chapel service and saw our speaker for the day. Doc Eshelman was a pastor and former NFL chaplain, who was founder and president of an organization called Sports World Ministries. Sports World was a group of professional athletes who spoke in schools and churches all over the world. Doc had been assigned the task of establishing the chapel program in the new league. He was a rugged-looking guy with a winning smile and a big voice.

I had never really listened to what chapel speakers had to say. And while Doc was speaking, my mind was really on the Tampa Bay Bandits. Somehow, though, his words broke through to my heart that day.

He was talking about the difference between "do" and "done" and why that's relevant to the Christian faith. Most people, he said, come to God with a list of things they think the have to do to get through the door. But Christ tells us that all the "do" has already been "done". When Jesus died on the cross for us and rose from the dead, the job was completed. Doc read John 1:12, which said, "Yet to all who did receive him, to those who believed in his name, he gave the right to become children of God." Being part of a family had always been important to me, so this caught my attention. He spoke about a religion based on rituals versus a lifestyle built on a relationship. "Religion," Doc said, "is man reaching for God, and relationship is God reaching for us."

I had never heard anything like this before. And, suddenly, I began to examine deep inside myself. I was where I had always dreamed of being, playing professional football, but it wasn't how I thought it would be. When success failed to satisfy me during the last couple of months, I had already begun looking for a "Plan B". A relationship with God – was that what I was missing? If God existed, and if all the stories in the Bible were true, then, I realized that maybe the emptiness that I was experiencing was because He wasn't there. Could it really be that all the fulfillment I thought would be mine through football, could be found in Christ?

I was willing to take that chance. At the conclusion of the service, Doc asked all of us to bow our heads. "If you agree that you're a sinner, and would like to begin a relationship with Jesus," Doc said, "I want you to raise your hand." I did it. It was that simple.

In the years since that day, I've come to understand that everybody's journey with Christ is different. I've known people who have asked Jesus into their lives and the immediately experienced radical changes. I didn't have that lightning-bolt encounter. After the chapel service, I walked out of the room and got ready to play football.

Maybe I didn't fully understood what happened to me during that chapel service in Tampa, but I knew what had happened was real. There weren't any overnight changes in my personality or the things that I did. During the next few months, I would go back to the old places and do the old things that always were so great, and they just weren't fun anymore. I knew that I didn't belong there in those locations and those situations. It seemed like someone had turned a light on, and I was seeing things completely different than I did before. I had been a blind man and, now, I could suddenly see everything around me.

That day, we avenged the earlier loss to the Bandits, beating them 24-10. I don't remember much about that game, or about my role in the victory. The chapel service, though, was still on my mind. I wanted to talk to someone about what had happened to me, but there didn't seem to be anyone around who was the right person to talk to. The subject of God, or Jesus, or a relationship with Him never came up. I called my family, and casually told them about what had happened to me, but they didn't seem to understand.

The season continued, and I started every game that year. We finished the regular season with a 15-3 record, by far, the best in the league. We cruised into the playoffs and faced the Chicago Blitz, led by Coach George Allen, in the first round. I had always been told that playoff football in the pros was a completely different game, and the contest against the Blitz proved it. We fought back from behind to force the game into overtime. We left it all on the field, and narrowly escaped with a 44-38 win.

A championship game – I hadn't been in one since I was in junior high school. And now, in my first professional season, my Philadelphia Stars would be taking on the Michigan Panthers in the finals. Through the first three quarters, the Panthers controlled the game. Going into the final quarter they had a 17-3 lead, and we knew we had to go to work. We moved to within with three points, and we were beginning to believe we could make the improbable comeback.

But Panthers quarterback Bobby Hebert had

a different idea. With three minutes left in the game, he threw a 48-yard touchdown pass to Anthony Carter to give them a 24-14 lead. As the clock ticked off the final seconds, we scored again, but our comeback wasn't quite enough. The Panthers won 24-22.

Losing never feels good. The Philadelphia Stars had a great season but just fell short of winning it all. We ended the season hungry for more.

The United States Football League had had an even more successful first year. Television ratings were up and the new league had won over a lot of fans with their exciting brand of football. The USFL had big plans for expanding. In the off season, they added franchises in Memphis, Jacksonville, Houston, San Antonio, Tulsa, and Pittsburgh. In order to fill the new teams' rosters, an expansion draft was held. The existing teams got to protect a few of their stars, but the rest of their squads were available to be selected.

On September 8, 1983, the draft was held in the USFL offices in New York City. By the end of the day, my entire perspective was about to change radically. I was now a San Antonio Gunslinger.

INSTANT REPLAY

This game against the Denver Gold in 1983's Week 1 was my first appearance in a regular season pro football game. ABC Sports selected it as their featured game, so it was the first USFL game and the first televised in USFL history https://vimeo.com/87830799

Our coach in Philadelphia was a young guy named Jim Mora. After leading the Stars to three USFL finals and two championships, he had a very successful career in the NFL. This may be his most famous moment though. As the head coach for the Indianapolis Colts, Coach Mora had this famous meltdown in a post-game press conference. https://vimeo.com/87868362

5 Deep In The Heart

"And I will give you a new heart, and I will put a new spirit in you. I will take out your stony, stubborn heart and give you a tender, responsive heart." Ezekiel 36:26

San Antonio, Texas, was so far off my radar screen that I had a hard time imagining what it would be like there. I suppose I expected cowboys, horses and the Wild West, so I was surprised at what I saw as I drove into town. The city was growing to almost a million in population, but had managed to keep an old historic charm about it.

I really wasn't looking forward to going to Texas. My agent was hesitant about me making the move to San Antonio. He thought we might be able to make another run at the NFL. But Lary Kuharich, who was one of my coaches at Temple, was the offensive coordinator for the Gunslingers, and he insisted that it was going to be great. He convinced me that San Antonio was the place for me.

I arrived there on Friday, January 13, 1984. The Gunslingers' training headquarters were at the beautiful old St. Anthony Hotel in downtown San Antonio. The St. Anthony was just a short stroll from both the Riverwalk and the Alamo.

I checked in, and made my way to my room. The room was small, with two twin beds that seemed cramped for big football players to get a good night's sleep on. As I decided which side of the room I was going to claim, the door swung open. A big guy with a big grin on his face said, "Hi, Rich! I'm Arland Thompson."

Arland, after playing for a few NFL teams,

They call it "The Cradle of Texas Liberty". The Alamo is San Antonio's best-known landmark.

The most beautiful place in San Antonio has to be the Riverwalk. The San Antonio River winds right through downtown and is a favorite place for tourists and the locals.

The St. Anthony Hotel right in the middle of downtown San Antonio was the headquarters for the Gunslingers' training camp. It was really much too nice for a bunch of big football players.

had spent the past season in the USFL with the Denver Gold. The Gunslingers had picked him up in the expansion draft, too, and he and I were slated to be the starting offensive guards. A native Texan, Arland filled me in on all the local color and warned me that once summer rolled around, San Antonio was going to get HOT! Adjusting to a new roommate can sometimes be tough, but, Arland and I immediately connected.

That evening, all my new teammates and I gathered for dinner. Some familiar faces were there, like Rick D'Amico, Frank Case and Brad Anae who had been with me with the Stars. And, I met some new friends, too. There was a good feeling in the room, and almost everybody just hung around that evening and got acquainted.

After the coaching staff gave us their expectations and encouragement, we headed for our rooms.

I crawled into the twin bed, and, like all the other lineman, I hung over the edges. My roommate made his way to his side, and turned off the lamp on the nightstand between our beds. It was quiet, and dark, and I was tired, so I started drifting into a good night's sleep. Just as I was fading, Arland called my name and woke me up

NEW HOME

This is Alamo Stadium, the home of the San Antonio Gunslingers.

The first thing they did when we got to San Antonio was take our pictures in our brand new blue, green and silver uniforms.

with a question.

"Hey, Rich."

"Yeah?"

"Have you ever asked Christ to come into your life?"

Suddenly, I was wide awake. My mind snapped back to that chapel service a few months before in the Tampa Bay locker room. I remembered the words that Doc Eshelman had spoken, the hunger I had in my heart, and the commitment that I had made that day. I sat up in my bed, and reached over and turned the lamp back on, and the room seemed bright as day.

"Yeah, I did that last year." Arland might not have expected that my answer was going to be this revelation that I was having. I began to tell him about my experience in Tampa, and as I talked about it, everything became even clearer for me. I understood, now, what God had begun in my life. Arland began to give me advice as to how I could nourish this new thing inside me. He assured me that he and other believers on this team would be there with me during my journey of faith.

"They asked me to be the team chaplain," Arland informed me. "So I'm going to be starting a Bible study. I really think it would be great if you were a part of it."

I had no idea about what I was committing to, but I let Arland know that I would be there.

I turned the light off again, and put my head back down on my pillow. I wasn't certain about where this was going, but I had a new course of direction for my life. It just felt right.

The next morning, I woke up early, got ready, and training camp began for real as we piled on the busses for the ride to Alamo Stadium. Team meetings, workouts, more meetings, then practice, filled the next few weeks. After playing on a team that played in the championship game, I wasn't sure how the Gunslingers were going to do in their first USFL season. But, I did become acquainted with a great group of guys. Some of them, God would use to make a huge impact on my life and my faith.

Danny Buggs was a tall, thin wide receiver who had been a solid player for the Washington Redskins. Off the field, he was a slow-talking, smooth-moving, peaceful guy, but on the field he was a real competitor. He had been a Christian for a number of years and brought to us stability and experience.

Mike Hagen was a new believer. He played for the Michigan Panthers in the USFL's first year. When his teammate, Bobby Hebert, told him the story of God's love through Jesus' sacrifice on the cross, Mike was eager to accept Christ as his Savior. He was a tough, strong fullback, with a big heart and a big smile.

Defensive back Mike Ulmer didn't have a lot to say. But he could run. God had brought his family through some very tough situations, and his faith was strong.

A huge, solid defensive lineman, Tommy Tabor, was a force on the football field. Off the field, he was the one of the gentlest, kindest guys

O LINE

Arland Thompson (left), Bill Winters (60) and I, circle our offensive line coach, Mike Barry.

I've ever known. He loved God and he loved people with all his heart.

Those players, along with Ray Waddy, Tony Armstrong, Jeff Chaffin, and many others made the San Antonio Gunslingers one of most solid, faith-filled group of athletes I've ever been around. God knew what He was doing in putting us together, because we were going to need each other through the next two seasons.

As with any expansion franchise, competing against other teams that had played together before made the Gunslingers automatic underdogs. The owner of the team was a Texas oilman who had a hefty financial statement at the time he had applied for a USFL franchise. When the bottom dropped out of the oil and gas industry in the next few months that followed, his wallet shrunk considerably. So, we didn't sign any "superstar" performers on the team except for possibly our rookie quarterback, Rick Neuheisel. Rick had made a name for himself when he led UCLA to a Rose Bowl victory the year before. With a rookie quarterback and a roster filled with players most people hadn't heard of, some of the press predicted that we wouldn't even win a game.

What we did have on the team were some pretty good football players who might not have had big names, but they had big hearts. Our head coach, Gil Steinke, was a Texas college football legend who had retired a few years earlier. He had coached Texas A&I University (now known as Texas A&M-Kingsville) to several small college national championships. What he brought to the Gunslingers was an amazing ability to see what was inside a football player. He always managed to recruit high school talent to A&I that the big college powerhouses overlooked. He found guys who might not have the size or the speed, but they wanted to play football. And our roster was full of that type, too.

We finished that 1984 season with a respectable 7-11 record, considering what was predicted for us. It was amazing to watch a group of guys come together and begin to build something. We depended on each other and knew that every player on that team had your back.

Away from the field, the Bible study that Arland had organized was thriving. Most of the guys on the team had at least visited the group. More important than the numbers, we were growing in our faith.

Something was happening inside me, too. As we studied together, the scriptures began to just jump off the pages at me. What had before been a confusing jumble of words, were now not only

QUICK TRIP

Because they were just three hours down the road, the Houston Gamblers were the Gunslingers' biggest rival. In this Gamblers' game, I'm headed for the bench. I'm hoping it was because our offense had just scored a touchdown.

making sense, but they were coming alive for me. I found peace there. I found wisdom there. I found fulfillment there.

Year two of the San Antonio Gunslingers began to get even rockier. The money crisis that our owner had been facing now began to affect us. Travel plans became more difficult, press interviews were more stressful, and our paychecks began to be late. Then, sometimes, there wouldn't be anything in the bank to cover them. It made for a stressful situation for everyone. Coach Steinke had "re-retired" before the season started, and our defensive coordinator, Jim Bates, had taken over as head coach. There was nobody I'd ever known as enthusiastic as Coach Bates, but, by mid-season, the stress began to get to him, too. He resigned, and Coach Steinke came out of retirement once again to lead the Gunslingers. We finished the year with a 5-13 record.

Around the rest of the USFL, things weren't going a whole lot better. My old team, the Stars were heading into their third championship game. This time though, their home was in Baltimore instead of Philadelphia. After some success with a spring schedule, some USFL owners felt it was time to challenge the NFL head-to-head. Donald Trump, the owner of the New Jersey Generals, led the push to move to a traditional fall football season. Most of the franchises though, found that NFL teams had their stadiums tied up during that time. So, the scramble was on to find new stadiums in new host cities, as well as new television network contracts. It became too big a task to handle.

The owners insisted that the NFL was a monopoly that was preventing them from doing business, so they filed suit against them. The jury decided that the NFL was guilty, but they awarded the USFL the sum of $1 in damages. It was going to take a bit more cash than that to pull the league out of financial trouble. So, the league that once held so much promise, closed its doors.

I felt so badly for my teammates who were now out of a job, and were suddenly scrambling to find work. The strength and encouragement that we drew from each other in San Antonio was keeping most everybody going. The Bible study continued, but from week-to-week, guys were moving on to other things and other places. Some went to NFL teams, and some were forced to find "real" jobs for the first time in their lives.

Despite all the uncertainty with football, I was actually excited about what God was doing in my life. I was prepared to say "yes" to whatever He had ahead. There were other Gunslinger players who had made themselves available to God, too. Mike Hagen joined a ministry called the Power Team. Danny Buggs, started an outreach to inner city youth in Atlanta. Mike Ulmer became a youth pastor in Texarkana, Texas. And many other teammates found a place to serve God and others.

No longer was I finding my fulfillment and sense of worth on a football field. I still loved it, and had the opportunity arisen for me to play again, I probably would have considered it. But I was a different person now. God had given me the vision to see that when I gave him my life, He gave me a new heart.

GUNSLINGER, FROM SAN ANTONE

For everyone who collects sports cards, these should certainly be on your "must have" list!

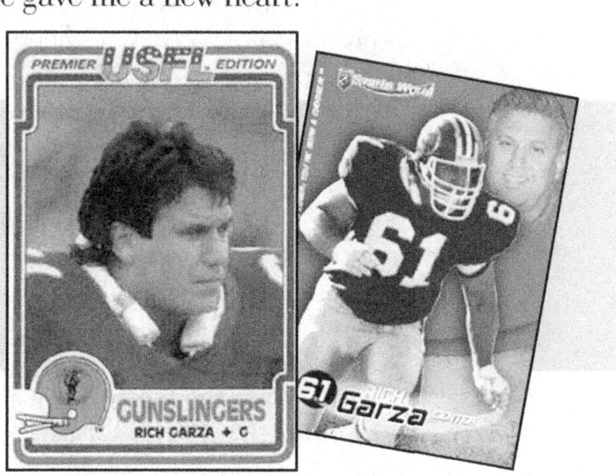

6 It's Not About Ability

"The Sovereign Lord has given me his words of wisdom, so that I know how to comfort the weary. Morning by morning he wakens me and opens my understanding to his will." Isaiah 50:4

At Temple University, I took Public Speaking 101 three times. But, I never finished a semester. Every time it was my turn to present a speech, I got so scared that I dropped the course. So after the third attempt, I decided speaking before an audience just wasn't for me. Why did a pro football player need to know how to make a speech anyway? And, after I retired from football, I had already decided that I would coach somewhere. The only speaking you had to do there was explaining the game to a bunch of guys. They had to listen to what you had to say, or you could get rid of them. Audiences in a big auditorium weren't quite so easy to dispose of.

On gameday, April 14, 1984, we gathered in the Jacksonville hotel meeting room of for our chapel service. I was surprised to see Doc Eshelman there, our guest speaker for the day. I hadn't seen Doc since that day I gave Christ control of my life, almost a year before. I was so anxious to share with him what had been happening to me during the past twelve months. I was listening to what he had to say, but, actually I was really focused on what I wanted to say to him after the meeting. I was sure it was something he needed to know.

"Hey, Doc," I said as I shook his hand. "I'm Rich Garza. I accepted Christ last year when you spoke at the Stars chapel in Tampa." He was smiling and seemed to be waiting to hear more, so I continued. "My life has changed so much since that day. I met some great guys in San Antonio and we're very involved in a Bible study. I've told my parents about what happened to me, and God is doing some great things in their lives, too. My faith in God is really growing."

Just as I was going to thank him for what he had said a year ago, Doc interrupted me. "That's great Rich! So, are you ready now to share that with others?" I wasn't quite sure what he had in mind, and I'm pretty certain that when he said that, I stuttered a bit and couldn't answer him. So, he continued. "We would love to have you share what God is doing in your life with some churches, schools, and other groups."

"Doc," I said, "you don't understand. I've never spoken to an audience in my whole life." And then I told him about what a miserable failure I had been in Public Speaking classes at Temple. He didn't even appear to be paying any attention to what I was saying.

"We'll train you. Be in Atlanta the first week of August. Sports World Ministries will be meeting there then. I'll give you the details later."

I never had a chance to argue with him about it. As far as Doc was concerned, I was on my way to Atlanta in August. It was a done deal.

Once I got to Atlanta, it was boot camp time. Doc's son, Paul, and Dennis Painter, a friend of Sports World who was on the staff of Campus Crusade for Christ, put me through all-day sessions of Bible study and speaker training. They had me put together, in detail, my story. I had to examine where I had been, where I was now, and where I was going. That intense week called for far more study time than I had ever done in a college classroom. But, it not only prepared me for future speaking opportunities, it gave me an even deeper insight into my relationship with Jesus. I was understanding more clearly the reality of that relationship, and the practical day-to-day journey that was before me. I understood that God wasn't promising that I, or every situation around me would be perfect, but I now had the tools to become what He wanted me to be.

Several weeks later, I got a call from Dennis Painter. He was going to be in York, Pennsylvania, about 100 miles from Bethlehem. He wanted me to meet him there. And he wanted me to be prepared to share my story at a school there.

When I started thinking that I had to do this standing in front of a crowd of people and talking, I began to feel those old jitters creeping in again. Dennis met me and reassured me that everything would be fine. When he introduced me, I would come to the podium and read my testimony, exactly what I had written down. That didn't sound too bad. I trusted Dennis, and I really felt that I wanted to tell people about the new and improved Rich Garza.

When I stood behind that podium, everything in front of me was a blur. I don't recall any faces in front of me, and the words I was reading sounded like a foreign language to my ears. I remember sweating and stuttering, and it seemed like I was standing up there forever. After I finished, I sat down and thought, "Man, what a disaster that was!" I never wanted to do that again and I was pretty sure that I would never be offered another opportunity anyway.

After the assembly was over and all the people and left, I reluctantly walked up to Dennis. "I'm so sorry for how terrible I was up there." I said, looking at the floor. "I know I really let you down."

He laughed at me. "Rich, you must not have been paying any attention at the end," he said. "Did you see the response from the students here? Look at this."

He handed me a stack of cards that had been passed out to the students at the beginning of the assembly. People had written on them about decisions that they had made that night. They were about how they had allowed Jesus into their lives and how they were new and clean inside. I was amazed.

"Rich," said Dennis, "it's not about your ability, it's about your availability. This is not about you. It's about God, and Him working through you."

Those words completely changed my life. There was such a release within me. And, immediately, I experienced a confidence like I'd never known before. It wasn't a confidence in what I could do. I knew who I was, and I clearly knew my failures and limitations. But, through Dennis's words, God spoke to my heart. I realized that He had made me who I was, and I was created for His reasons and His purposes. He knew even better than me my faults and weaknesses, and it wasn't about that at all. I learned, at that moment, that God wanted to use me as I was. My ability or lack of it wasn't the important thing. My availability to Him was all that mattered. When I said, "Yes, God, use me," that's all He needed to hear.

In the years that have followed that day in York, I've had the opportunity to share my story with more than three million people. I still know I may not be the best communicator there is, but I also know that that doesn't make any difference to God. What's important is that I make myself available to any opportunity He creates for me. In churches, schools, auditoriums, locker rooms, or prison yards, I belong to God, so I give Him my voice and my words. I depend on Him to make me aware of the individuals I share my story with, to give me the words that He wants me to say.

I tell the people that I speak to, something that I would like to share with you now. Just like Rich Garza, God has created you for a purpose. It may not be that you're supposed to speak before groups of people. But whatever it is, He has equipped you to do it. And when you realize, like I did, that it's not about you, but it's all about Him, then that's exactly the place that He can begin to use you.

JUST FOLLOWING INSTRUCTIONS

I wasn't the first guy to try to back out of a speaking engagement. In Exodus 4, God called Moses to lead the Children of Israel out of slavery in Egypt. Moses was certain that God was making a huge mistake.

"But Moses pleaded with the LORD, 'O Lord, I'm not very good with words. I never have been, and I'm not now, even though you have spoken to me. I get tongue-tied, and my words get tangled.'
Then the LORD asked Moses, 'Who makes a person's mouth? Who decides whether people speak or do not speak, hear or do not hear, see or do not see? Is it not I, the LORD? Now go! I will be with you as you speak, and I will instruct you in what to say.'"

7 Pizza, Fajitas, Tamales and Love

"There are three things that amaze me – no, four things that I don't understand: how an eagle glides through the sky, how a snake slithers on a rock, how a ship navigates the ocean, how a man loves a woman." Proverbs 30:18-19

After the Gunslingers' owner had missed a couple of paychecks, free, all-you-can-eat pizza sounded like a pretty good deal. I was selected Player of the Week, along with Nick Mike-Mayer, our kicker, who also happened to be a Temple grad, so we got to meet the fans and sign autographs at Fargo's Pizza. The restaurant manager set us up at a table in the front of the dining room, and with a plateful of pizza in front of us (the first of several we had that night) we talked to the fans there. When I wasn't autographing photos, I was stuffing pizza in my mouth, and looking around the restaurant at all the people that were there.

I happened to notice a very pretty young lady seated at a table on the other side of the room. She was engaged in conversation with the others at her table, and didn't seem really very eager to meet the football players who were there.

I wasn't looking for romance that night at the pizza place. I really didn't have time for it. My priority was, first, my faith. My relationship with Christ had become such a fulfilling part of my life that I was pursuing it with my whole heart. And right behind that came football. I had dreamed about this time my entire life, so I was going make every minute count. I hadn't even gone out on a date for almost two years, but I figured there would be time for that later.

But there was just something about that girl there that night that captured my attention. She had such a beautiful and sincere smile. I tried over and over again to catch her eye, but she never looked my way.

The manager was going from table-to-table, encouraging the patrons to meet the Gunslinger players that were appearing there. He came to the girl's table, and while he was talking to them, she looked over at me. When she got up and began to walk toward our table, my first thought was to make sure I didn't have any pizza on my mouth.

When she walked up to where I was, I introduced myself and she told me her name was Jan Montoya. I thought it would be good to strike up a conversation with her. After all, that's why I was there – to meet the fans! We talked for a few minutes and I found a little more about her.

ONCE UPON A TIME

This is how it all started! Here's the ad that appeared in the stadium program, announcing that I would be signing autographs at Fargo's Pizza.

Then I asked, "Would you like to go to the game this weekend?" She said, "Sure! That sounds great." "If you give me your phone number," I replied, "I'll call you and let you know how you can pick up the ticket."

I didn't know how she would take that, but she gave me her number. I later found out that it was her number at work. She wasn't about to give a guy she just met her home phone.

I called Jan that week and told her who she needed to contact at the ticket office. Then I told her that I would like it if she met me after the game in front of the locker room so I could say hello. She said she would be there, but there was always that chance that she would just leave after the game was over.

So as I walked out of the locker room that evening, I guess I was somewhat surprised to see her standing there.

When I walked over to her, she thanked me for the ticket and told me that she had a great time. We exchanged some small talk, then, I said, "Hey, I'm really hungry. Do you want to go somewhere to get a bite to eat?"

I was definitely happy when she said that she would like to go with me. I don't think I really considered it a date. When most of your meals are spent in the company of big sweaty guys, it was just nice to sit across the table from a female. And it didn't hurt that she was very pretty, too.

We made our way to the Mercado area of downtown San Antonio and walked through the doors of Mi Tierra Café. It's a San Antonio landmark, and, I knew that because it was open twenty-four hours, we would have plenty of time to talk. And I also knew that no matter how late we arrived, Mi Tierra would always have plenty of fajitas for us to dine on.

Had I been worried about keeping a conversation going with Jan, that would have been solved immediately. She began asking question after question about what made me tick. I answered her honestly and openly, and she, too, was truthful about things in her life that she was passionate about and things she was beginning to question. Even with all the interesting conversation, I still managed to finish off a pound of delicious fajitas.

I could tell that Jan was someone who was searching for more in here life – more peace, more fulfillment, and a greater purpose. I understood that completely. I had been there, too, and found out that Christ was the answer. At one point, she asked me how I was able to keep my composure and keep playing even though we were missing paychecks. I told her there was only one thing that kept my motivated to put everything on the line, week after week. "Colossians 3:23 is my motivation," I told her. "'And whatever you do, do it heartily, as to the Lord and not to men.' I don't play football for a paycheck, I play it as unto the Lord."

I had a great evening with Jan, and even though I did want to see her again, I also felt like I had an opportunity to help her discover what she was searching for. "Would you like to go to church with me next Sunday?" I asked. She said that she would like that and this time she gave me her home phone number. I called her early in the week and we talked about going to church together. She seemed surprised that we would be going to a Protestant church, though. I suppose that the more she began to think about it, the more hesitant she got, not knowing whether she should go to something other than a Catholic Church. So when I called her on Saturday to confirm when I'd be picking her up, I got no answer. And I called again, again and again, and she never picked up the phone.

I didn't give up very easily. The next week, I called Jan again, and she answered this time.

SWEETHEARTS

Here we are in 1985, just a few months before we were married. As pretty as my wife is, she's even more beautiful on the inside. I'm so blessed!

I can't believe we were so young! My beautiful wife, Jan, and I were on our way to my brother Ron's wedding in Pennsylvania.

"We have a team Bible study that I go to every week," I said. "There are other ladies there, too, and I'd really like for you to go with me." She agreed to go, as long as she didn't have to answer any questions or read any scripture aloud.

The next night, I picked Jan up and took her to the Bible study. I could tell that she was bit intimidated by all the huge guys in the room, but when she met some of the players' wives and girlfriends, she felt a little less out of place.

After the study was over, I was anxious to get her input about it. "I felt very welcome," Jan said. "The thing that amazed me was how gentle and kind those big men are. I think I expected them to be loud and rough. But, I saw Danny Buggs with his little boy holding on to him, and with his baby girl in his arms, and it was just so sweet."

We pulled up in front of Jan's house, and she talked about how much it moved her to see a group of people so committed to God. Even, if they faced difficult circumstances, they were peaceful. It was something that she was really hungry for.

So, it got quiet for a moment, and I asked her very simply, "Are you ready?" I guess that question could have been interpreted many ways, but she seemed to know exactly what I meant. Right there in my car, in front of Jan's house, I explained to her how she could have that peace and fulfillment.

I told her that God loved her so much and had a great plan for her life. But, she needed to agree with God the she, like everyone else, is a sinner that needs to ask Him to forgive her. "Jesus died in your place," I said, "as a sacrifice for our sin. We need to acknowledge that we can only make things right with God by accepting His death on the cross and resurrection as our only hope." And the I asked her to pray with me and accept Jesus as her Savior and her Lord. When we finished praying, Jan told me that she felt like a huge load had been lifted from her shoulders. "I have peace like I've never had before," she said.

It was a wonderful moment for both of us, and there was no better way to begin a relationship. It just seemed like we belonged together from that moment on. I guess we didn't have the traditional type of courtship. Most of our "dates" were getting together with Mike and Ann Hagen and Mike and Sharon Ulmer, for dinner, fellowship and Bible study. Those were precious times for both us that built a strong foundation for our marriage and family through all these years.

Just a few months later, on New Year's Eve, 1985, I was with Jan in the kitchen while we stood around the stove loading our plates with tamales. To me, for some reason, that seemed like a perfect time to ask her to marry me. To be honest, I don't guess I really asked her, I told her. "We need to decide on a date to get married," I said.

March 1, 1986, turned out to be the day. There was never any doubt in my mind then, and never any since, that Jan Montoya was a gift from God to me. When she became Jan Garza, it was the happiest day of my life.

From almost the first day of our married life, I had speaking engagements to fulfill and we went out on the road together all over the country.

And that was what our life was like until God blessed our lives with our beautiful family. It's been so amazing watching together as Kelly, Richie, Danny and David have grown up and become such great people. Jan stayed at home with the kids while I talked to people about Jesus. And now, again, since the kids have all left the house, we get to share those moments of being together once again.

We have grown even closer as the years have gone by and we've grown closer to God. When God established marriage and families, he paved the way for the most incredible relationships that a person can enjoy on this earth. I'm so thankful he blessed me with that gift.

THE GARZAS

God has blessed me with such a beautiful family. From the left front and moving clockwise is my daughter Kelly, my oldest son Richie, me, Jan, Danny and David.

8 Great People, Great Friends

"A man's gift makes room for him, and brings him before great men."
Proverbs 18:16

When I was younger, I never could have imagined that I would spend my life going all over the world, telling others about Christ. I never thought that I would be able to get my eyes off my own inadequacies and my failures in speech classes, to speak before millions of people.

My calling, sharing the Good News of Jesus Christ, has been a gift from God. Every time I stand before a group of people, I think about what Dennis Painter said to me after I spoke to that first group. It's not about my abilities, anything I am or have been. It's all because I said "Yes" to Jesus. I just made myself available.

A part of the gift that God gave me has been the opportunity to meet so many amazing people. Some of them were leaders of nations, noted preachers and pastors, and great athletes. Some were people that you wouldn't recognize if you passed them on the streets, but their stories of courage and what they've overcome amaze me.

In the next few chapters of this book, I wanted to speak specifically to several groups of people into whose lives God has given me a voice. I want to share my heart with teens, parents, prison inmates and athletes. I wanted you to know what

I think about when I think about you, and what I pray for when I pray for you.

But before that, to conclude this chapter, I wanted to create for you a photo album that will show you some of the meaningful moments I've spent with some very special people. I couldn't begin to include every one of them, but these are some that we captured in photos.

AMERICAN HEROES

Among the greatest privileges of my life are the opportunities I have to speak to members of the military, because they're the real heroes. These young men are in training at the military academy in Harlingen, Texas.

KEVIN WILLIS

Kevin Willis had an incredible 24-year NBA career. He was a vital part of the San Antonio Spurs' 2003 championship season.

JOHN MACARTHUR
Jan and I had an opportunity to meet Pastor John MacArthur. *Christianity Today* magazine named him one of the most influential preachers of this time.

THE ADMIRAL
The Spurs' David Robinson was named one of the Top 50 all-time greatest players in NBA history. For me, he has been a great friend and one of the finest Christian men I have ever known.

Meeting President George Bush was one of the greatest honors of my entire life. He is such a genuine, humble man. This took place at an Anti-Drug Rally in Lancaster, Pennsylvania in 1988.

NBA stars

Jeremy Lin (right) and James Harden (left) not only lead the Houston Rockets on the court, but they are also a vital part of the team's chapel.

I always look forward to seeing Kevin Durant, one of the NBA's brightest young stars. Whenever the Spurs play the Oklahoma City Thunder, I'm sure to see him at chapel.

TOM LANDRY

Jan and I were thrilled to meet Tom and Alicia Landry. Coach Landry led the Dallas Cowboys to two Super Bowl championships. His 250 wins rank him third among all-time NFL coaches. His life was a shining example, as he dedicated all that he did to God's glory.

MARK JACKSON

Following a great NBA career, Mark Jackson has quickly become one of the league's top coaches. In the 2012-2013 season, Mark led the Golden State Warriors into the second round of the NBA playoffs. It was the first time the Warriors had made the playoffs in six years.

ROGER MASON, JR.

While he was playing for the Spurs, Roger Mason Jr. was a vital member of our chapel. He is currently playing for the Miami Heat.

JOE KRALIK

San Antonio Texans' wide receiver Joe Kralik was a star on the University of Washington's national championship team in 1991.

PARTNERS AND SUPPORT

Kelly McAndrew is the founder and President of Soldiers For Faith, a ministry that has reached millions with the message of Christ. I'm so grateful that God has given me an opportunity to partner with him.

Jan's father and mother, Nestor and Gloria Montoya, have always been there for my family and me. My father-in-law passed away and I miss him very much.

This is my pastor, David Walker and his wife Shirley. Pastor Walker has been an amazing strength to my life and my ministry. Alamo City Church provides a solid foundation for the entire Garza family.

Jerry and Caroline Balswick are my mentors, counselors, supporters and friends. I'm so blessed that they are a part of my life.

God has placed so many significant people in my life. Among those are couples like Cas and Susan Staffel and Dan and Debbie Rodriguez. I depend on them for their support, their prayers and their counsel.

9 To the Teens

"Don't let anyone look down on you because you are young, but set an example for the believers in speech, in conduct, in love, in faith and in purity." I Timothy 4:12

When I get to talk to students, that's absolutely my best time ever. There's nothing more alive than a room full of high schoolers, and when I'm with you guys, I feel like I'm sixteen again.

While I was growing up in Pennsylvania, every adult seemed to have some advice for me. They all said something like, "Rich, the choices you make in your life will make you or break you." I don't think I really appreciated or fully understood what they were telling me back then. But it's funny that, now that I'm an adult, I feel like I need to tell you the very same thing.

A few years ago, I was talking to a group of teens and I got on a roll. Something just popped into my head. "You're not born a winner or a loser," I said. "You're born a chooser."

Life is all about making choices. It starts when you're a baby and you choose to stand up and walk because that makes things a lot better than when you're crawling on the floor. Then, for the rest of your life you choose one path over the other. You decide to do something because you think it might benefit you, or just because you think it would be fun. There are a lot of factors that influence those choices we make during our lives.

Kids that make bad choices are listening to

GETTING REAL
There's nothing better than having an opportunity to talk to teenagers! I love how honest they are, how they challenge me, and how they ask so many relevant questions.

the wrong voices. You know the people I'm talking about. Instead of listening to those who love them most, like their parents, ministers, teachers and coaches, they look for advice from people who are only concerned with their own self interests.

The big challenge is sorting out all those voices. Think about who you're listening to these days. Are they talking to you because they have a $50 concert ticket they want you to buy? Have they just released some new music they want you to download? Or, do they have a new movie or television show that needs to have the ratings boosted? What about people you see every day? Are they wanting you around so they'll feel better about the bad things they're doing? Or, worse than that, are they counting on you to take the fall if they get in trouble? If what they're talking about is all about their needs, then following their voice is not going to get you where you want to be.

The smartest thing you could ever do is to realize that God has surrounded you with other voices that will encourage you to be everything you're meant to be. They won't hold you back from making all the right choices. They want the very best for you, and they'll let you know it when you're settling for less than that. They're the voices you need to hear.

So how do you make sure you're listening to the right people? Begin by choosing to spend your time with the ones who are making right decisions themselves. In I Corinthians 15:33, Paul made it pretty clear. He said, "Do not be deceived: bad company corrupts good morals." If you're really wanting to make the right choices and do the right things, then stay away from bad company. The good company encourages you, the bad company makes you doubt yourself. The good company has dreams and goals for their future. The bad company lives only for the thrill of this moment. The good company is respectful of others. The bad company tears others down and hurts them. The good company helps you step up and shine. The bad company holds you down. Find the good company around you and spend your time with them.

There's another choice you make that will influence you. It's the choice of what you put inside your body. I won't apologize for the fact that I am a strong believer that the use of alcohol and other drugs can destroy anything positive that's going on in your life. We hear about the dangers of driving while intoxicated, but that's only the beginning. Every forty seconds, someone commits suicide, and alcohol are found to contribute in almost 30% of them. That is pure destruction. Alcohol may seem like the least harmful, but it doesn't create a high. It's a depressant, and that pushes people over the edge. Absolutely no permanent good comes from alcohol and other drugs. Choosing to play with them is one of the biggest risks you can ever take.

There's one other thing I want you to think about. You're not an island. By that I mean that every choice you make affects other people, too. It's like throwing a rock in a lake, and seeing the ripples spread out further and further. Every choice you make will touch everyone around you now, and everyone that will be a part of your future. Your family, your friends, your school, your sports team, your community, and your world are all impacted. Your choice makes that influence positive and life-giving or negative and destructive.

I want you to know that I believe in you. You are God's creation and He has a purpose and a mission exclusively for you. I can't wait to hear about it as you change your world for Him!

WORLD CHANGERS

Being with teens is life-giving for me. These guys have their whole lives ahead of them, and when they are surrendered to Christ, they will change their worlds.

10 To the Parents

"Children are a heritage from the LORD, offspring a reward from him. Like arrows in the hands of a warrior are children born in one's youth. Blessed is the man whose quiver is full of them." Psalm 127:3-5

I have no greater honor on this earth than to be called "Dad" by Kelly, Richie, David and Danny Garza. Through great times and tough times, I've always loved them and I've always been proud of them. They are becoming people who truly follow God and that brings Jan and I so much joy.

The blessing of being a parent is one of God's greatest gifts. It's not an easy job, but that's nothing compared to the joy you receive as you watch them grow.

In Deuteronomy 6, God gave parents specific directions about how they should handle their responsibilities:

"And these words which I command you today shall be in your heart. You shall teach them diligently to your children, and shall talk of them when you sit in your house, when you walk by the way, when you lie down, and when you rise up."

God wants us to teach our kids about Him as we're going through our everyday events of our lives. We can't sit our kids down on the chair and preach to them. That's just not effective.

What the scripture sets out for us is that, while we're building our relationship with the children – while we're around the house, or at the dinner table, or at the park, we demonstrate God to them. I once heard a wise man of God say that if we didn't build a relationship with our kids, we're sure to have rebellion. Relationship requires us to invest time. And, as we spend time with them, we talk to them about Who God is, what Jesus did for us, and how God wants us to live our lives.

But notice what God says first in that Deuteronomy passage. The first thing we have to be sure of, as parents, is that God's word and God's ways are in our hearts. When I was growing up, my mom and dad couldn't teach me anything that they didn't already know themselves. We have to be experiencing God today in order to answer our kids' questions.

And they do have so many questions.

"Why does our family believe this?"

"Why do we stay away from some things?"

"Why is this important to us?"

"Why does our family pray, reach out to others, go to church?"

We sow the seeds of faith and truth in their hearts concerning these things, so when they have questions later, they know to turn to God and His Word for answers.

There's another important principle of parenting that we should know. We find it in Proverbs 22:6:

"Train up a child in the way he should go, and when he is old he will not depart from it."

The word "train" is important for us to notice. We don't beat Godly things into them. We don't simply raise kids and hope it will happen, either. We train them. That means we carefully direct their steps without limiting their options. We uncover our children's gifts and abilities, their interests and their passions, and we help them narrow them so that they can discover God's specific mission for their lives.

This parenting thing can be pretty intimidating when we look at the depth and the breadth of our responsibilities. But I can assure you from my own experience, God gives you the grace and wisdom you need as you put Him first and seek Him every moment. So, this is what's important – know God and know His Word, and learn to apply it day by day. Then work to build that relationship with your kids, spend time with them, talk to them about God and His Word. Speak life and faith into them. He honors that commitment!

HERITAGE Here's another picture of my family. One of the greatest privileges that God has given me is to partner with Jan to parent these wonderful kids. From left to right is Richie, Kelly, Jan, Danny and David.

11 To the Inmates

"For the LORD hears the cries of the needy; he does not despise his imprisoned people." Psalm 69:33

Back in 1988, I had an opportunity to speak to the guys at the California Youth Authority in Stockton, California. It was the first time I had been with a group of inmates, and I learned a lot from them. Since that time, I've been to prisons throughout the United States, and I've been with thousands of inmates. Almost all of you, when you get real with me, have expressed one thing you're feeling deep down inside you. You all feel hopeless.

I've been with the prisoners on death row in Raleigh, North Carolina, and Huntsville, Texas. Their sentence leaves them with no hope. Men and women who are incarcerated because of an addiction problem can't find a way out. Teens who have been in tough situations at home just want to find someplace, any place, to belong.

I've never been an inmate before, so I'm not able to identify with your experience. When I visit a prison, and they close the door behind me, I know that in a few hours, I'll be getting out. I can identify with your feeling of hopelessness, though. I've been in situations where I felt like the pain would never end, and I didn't have any answers.

I want to share with you my favorite word. It's a word that turned my life around, and, even now, when I feel like I'm not up to the task, it

HOPE

Whenever I speak to inmates, I always want to leave them with a message of hope. They suffer through some unbearable times of despair, and they need to know that God is there for them to give them grace and mercy.

gives me hope. The word is "***whosoever***" I found that word in my Bible. Almost all of you have heard the verse from John 3:16:

"For God so loved the world, that he gave his only begotten Son, that ***whosoever*** *believeth in him should not perish, but have everlasting life."*

"***Whosoever***" is a word we don't hear too often these days. It means ***whoever*** believes in Him will live forever with Him. The Bible uses that word a lot. Acts 2:21 says:

"And it shall come to pass, that **whosoever** *shall call on the name of the Lord shall be saved."*

There are a lot of you reading this right now that believe the things you've done that put you here, all the mistakes that you've made in your life, that God could never forgive you for them. You think that the tangled mess that your life has become through all the ways you have hurt people and people have hurt you, is hopeless.

Let me tell you again my favorite word – "***whosoever***". ***Whoever*** believes in Jesus Christ, ***whoever*** trusts that He will forgive, ***whoever*** wants to have a relationship with Him is welcome. There's nothing too bad that He won't forgive it. He's not surprised or shocked at anything you've done in the past, because He already knows it. It just doesn't matter because He still loves you.

He never promises that if you decide to follow Him then you'll never have any more problems.

If you put your trust in Him, you'll probably still have to serve out your sentence, because having a relationship with Jesus isn't magic. It's real and it fills that emptiness you feel inside right now. There are thousands of men and women who are in prisons throughout this country who have decided to follow Him. They may still be living behind bars, but they have changed. God has done something inside them. They've become a part of God's family.

Most of all, what that relationship offers you is hope. When God forgives you, it's forever. You may live to be 100 here on earth, but someday for you, and me, and all of us, this life will end. And because we have been forgiven, our hope is found in the fact that God promises that we will live with Him always.

I want you to know that I think of you and I pray for you. I know there's nothing easy about being where you are. My prayer for you is that you'll decide to follow Jesus Christ and receive the hope He has for you. And if you've already done that, I'm asking God to give you the strength to hold on to Him. And don't forget that God has promised that He's holding on to you too. It's great to know that you and I belong to Him, and He said He would never let anybody or anything take us out of His hands.

BILL GLASS

Bill Glass was a legendary NFL defensive lineman, who starred for eleven seasons with the Detroit Lions and Cleveland Browns. As great as his football career was, it doesn't come close to the impact that he has had on the lives of inmates in more than 40 years of prison ministry.

12 To the Athletes

"Don't you realize that in a race everyone runs, but only one person gets the prize? So run to win! All athletes are disciplined in their training. They do it to win a prize that will fade away, but we do it for an eternal prize." I Corinthians 9:24-25

I've been involved in sports my entire life. Throughout the entire time I was growing up, I wanted to be a professional football player, and I'm thankful I had that opportunity.

My teams always seemed like a family to me. When I think about the guys I played with, I consider many of them to be like brothers. To me, that was the greatest thing about being an athlete – the kinship I had with my teammates. In my own family, we always talked about "otherness". We tried to instill an attitude that our family was all about each other. We wanted each person in our house to think about each other before we though about ourselves, putting their needs ahead of our own. I suppose that was something I got from sports. There was such a great feeling about belonging to that team, about all the other guys who "had my back".

It's a shame that we've seen a "me-attitude" among so many athletes recently. It's certainly not an attitude that causes their teammates to have confidence in them. The important aspects of trust and unity that make a team so successful can't be built on selfishness.

As an athlete, you've been given, on so many levels, incredible opportunities to affect other people's lives. You have a unique platform from

FCA HUDDLES
The guy on the track is me, speaking to thousands of students in McAllen, Texas. This was a gathering of Fellowship of Christian Athletes' huddles from all over South Texas and the Rio Grande Valley.

which you can demonstrate that "otherness". Because I was an athlete, I've had the opportunity to speak to millions of people. No matter how young or old you are, whether you're playing sports in middle school, or high school, or college, or the pros, you've been put into the spotlight. You have a chance to be a real leader, a positive influence, an inspiring voice.

If you're a Christian, I can assure you that your place in athletics is an opportunity that God has given you to share your faith with others, including your teammates. Because of that platform, you have people's attention, and you can speak life-giving words that will challenge them to find Christ.

But it's not just words that are important. Words are empty if you're not demonstrating Jesus in the way you live your life. What you do, or what you don't do, speak even louder than what you say you are.

It may sound too simple, but your biggest challenge in keeping your life in order is how you use your time. When you're an athlete, so much of your time is taken up with practicing and playing your sport, that, during down time, you feel like just totally letting everything go. Rest is good, of course, but make sure that you make your faith your top priority. Read the Bible, talk with God and serve other people. Don't let the relaxation become something that draws you away from your focus.

I have the privilege of being team co-chaplain with Harvey Pendleton for the San Antonio Spurs for seventeen years, so I've been able to talk to many NBA players around the league. When I speak to them, I always try to remind them what Joshua 1:8 says:

"Keep this Book of the Law always on your lips; meditate on it day and night, so that you may be careful to do everything written in it. Then you will be prosperous and successful."

Meditate, think about, the Word of God. In the middle of a losing streak, in the fourth quarter of a close game, when an opponent is getting on your nerves, you can recall what God's Word says about the moment. If you know Him, you'll find some incredible strength to draw from.

For those of you who aren't believers yet, I wish I could tell you that becoming a Christian will assure that you'll have success in your sport. But I just can't. What I can promise is that with Jesus Christ, you can have peace in tough times. You'll have a sense of belonging that even surpasses being on the team, and you'll be certain that the One that always has your back, never failing, is Jesus, Himself.

LONGHORN CHAPEL FOR ALAMO BOWL

When the University of Texas Longhorns played in the Valero Alamo Bowl game in San Antonio, I was invited to speak at the team chapel.

FCA GROUPS IN OHIO

I was invited to speak to this Fellowship of Christian Athlete's group in Ohio. It was so uplifting to be able to pray with this group of teens from high schools all over the area.

13 Finding Your Vision

"But blessed are your eyes for they see, and your ears for they hear; for assuredly, I say to you that many prophets and righteous men desired to see what you see, and did not see it, and to hear what you hear, and did not hear it." Matthew 13:16-17

I still remember every detail of that day in the hotel in Tampa when I asked Christ to come into my life. That day, and every day since then, God has done some amazing things in my life. And because of that, I have such a hunger within me for you, and everyone else I meet, to know Him too.

Earlier in this book, I compared my experience to a blind man who suddenly could see things clearly. I want to use this outline of the blind man's story to help you get your testimony down. This simple outline has helped me tremendously as I have made myself "available" to God. I encourage you to think about your answers to the following questions and then write your answers down. Your answers are your testimony, and you too will be able to say God, I'm "available".

I was blind.

What's my heritage?

My family upbringing, my parents, siblings, extended family

My education and interests (sports, band, etc.)

My employment

My religious background; church, etc.

Who am I? Where am I?

How did I feel about my life as I grew up?

What areas of my life are difficult right now?

Have I invited Christ to come in my life and lead me?

How do these Bible verses affect me?

Matthew 5:3

Romans 3:23

Psalm 51:5

I met Jesus.

Who first shared Jesus' story with me?

Where was I when I first heard the story?

What do I remember about what was said?

What was my response to what I heard?

What do these Bible verses say to me?

John 1:12

Romans 10:13

John 3:16

Ephesians 2:8-10

Now I see.

How has knowing God changed my life?

Has it changed desires that I once had?

How do I feel about my old ways before I came to Christ?

Do I want to be the same places as always?

Do I put the things in my body that I used to?

Do I want to hang around the same old crowd?

What input do I have into my life right now?

Who do I listen to?

Where do I get advice?

What do I read?

1. Newton 10th
2. Loved how you told about how
you cared.
3. I needed to hear that
people care, strangers even

, 8 Newton

It was awsome, really learned alot
THANKS
I NEEDED THIS TALK THANK YOU!! Please
Moms Death - (OD) Come Back!

Miami East 8th
Great: Very life Changing for me
Made me decide to Change my
ways of living life. Not using
those things to have a good
time at a party.

How do these Bible verses affect my perspec tive today?

II Corinthians 5:17
Ephesians 2:10
Romans 12:1-2

How can I share this with others?

I need to write this all down
I should read over what I wrote
I need to remind myself about it often
I can share it?

Churches
Prisons
With younger groups
Sunday school classes
Schools

How can I be more aware of others' needs?
What can I do to be available to others?
How can I be a better listener?
What can I do to help those less fortunate than I am?

The most important thing that you can do is to realize that, even before you were born, God had a purpose and a plan for you. Even then, He wanted to have a relationship with you, and He wanted you to be a part of His family. He's not mad at you, and He hasn't given up on you. His plan for you was put into action when Jesus gave His life on the cross. He defeated death and the grave and He lives again to give you that opportunity to have a relationship with God.

It's done already. There's nothing else you have to do but agree that you're a sinner and, by faith, receive Him as your Lord and Savior. Then, just let Him know that you're available.

School or Organization: Kelly High School

Name: ______ Grade: 10th

comments I hard you speek at sikestion in 8th grade. I havn't done drugs seens then or befor but I kept my promice to you that I wouldn't in the future & I promice agin not to. Thanx for being there to lead the way.

senseroly,
Summer J.

continue on other side

School or Organization: Robert C. Byrd High School

Name: ______ Grade: 11

comments
Thank you. You have talked me out of suicide.

continue on other side

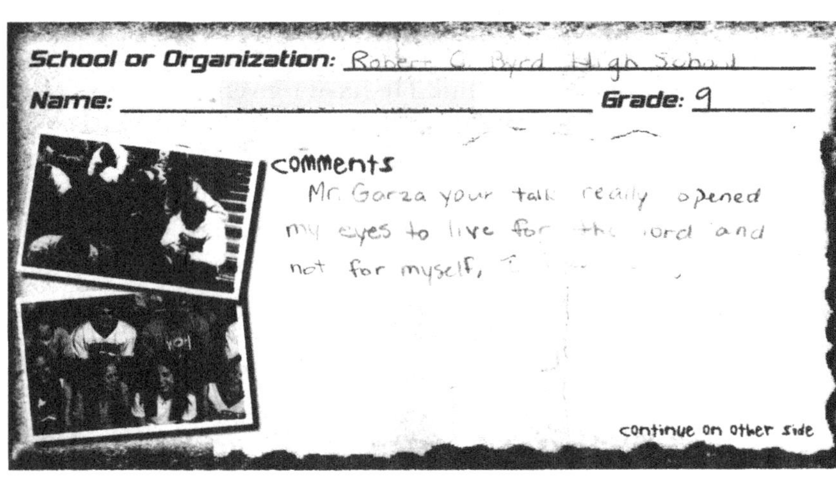

School or Organization: Robert C. Byrd High School

Name: ______ Grade: 9

comments
Mr. Garza your talk really opened my eyes to live for the lord and not for myself,

continue on other side

School or Organization: Poplar Bluff High School.

Name: ______________ Grade: 10

comments

My friend that I cared for very much committed suicide. I wish I could tell him about Jesus. I missed my chance, but I know I can save others.

continue on other side

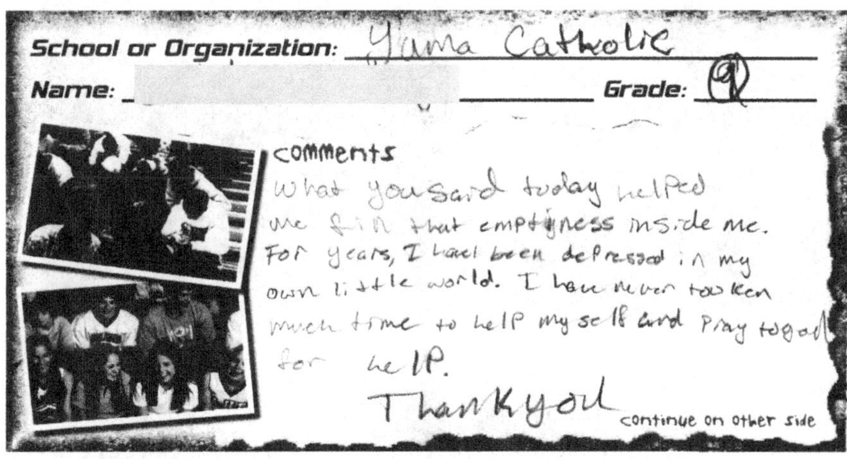

School or Organization: Yuma Catholic

Name: ______________ Grade: 9

comments

What you said today helped me fill that emptyness inside me. For years, I have been depressed in my own little world. I have never tooken much time to help my self and pray to god for help.

Thank you

continue on other side

School or Organization:

Name:

Do you have a question, a comment, or a commitment that you would like to share with Rich?

comments

Contact him via the email address below:

rgarza@soldiersforfaith.com

Afterword

In October, 2013, I was honored to be inducted into the National Hispanic Sports Hall of Fame. I'm grateful to God for that blessing, and to those who selected me. Along with me, Robert Quiroga of San Antonio was also inducted. I first met Robby, the tall young man to my right, when he was a standout receiver at Holmes High School. He was a part of the Fellowship of Christian Athletes group there where I spoke on several occasions. He later became a record-setting performer at Baylor University and in the Arena Football League.

Aknowledgements

My lord and Savior JESUS CHRIST Who did for me what I could not do for myself.

Everyone mentioned in this book.

Paul Eshleman, Sports World Ministry board. Corky Trebilcock, Mike Hockett, Bob Plunk, Jim Blankemeyer, Bob Blankemeyer, Ezra Clemons, Pat Stillman, Mike Cobb, Ken Johnson, Ken Ellis, Jack Krage, Dennis Norton, Dan Enger, Bob Nations, Joe Perri, Mic Cottom,Tom Radisak, Dave Kendal, Steve Lantz, John Brooks, Steve Roberts, Jim Faulk, Bill Robertson, Larry Sholink, Jim Wester, Albert Beidenharn, San Antonio Spurs.

Thousands of Principals, coaches, wardens, pastors, business owners, ministries who have opened their doors for me to speak.

My home church, Alamo City Church.

All who pray and give so I can go.

Special thanks to Greg and Martha Singleton for helping me get this book done!

Made in the USA
Coppell, TX
01 March 2026